Shipping Container Homes

A guide to shipping container homes, including plans, design ideas, and much more!

Table of Contents

Introduction 1

Chapter 1: What Is A Shipping Container Home? 3

Chapter 2: Licenses & Laws 8

Chapter 3: Sourcing Containers 13

Chapter 4: How To Build A Home 18

Chapter 5: Pros & Cons 28

Chapter 6: The Many Choices 33

Conclusion 39

Introduction

The idea of shipping containers being turned into homes is relatively new, but it is a growing fashion. It offers cheap, flexible, environmentally sound but stable and practical solutions to the housing challenges faced by many.

This book will give you a clear and detailed insight into this trend. It will help you understand the process of creating your own shipping container home, or for those with a more abstract interest in the topic, it will offer handy information for your consideration.

Like many trends that come and go (although, this one is so clever that we expect it to turn from trend to lifestyle), information about this subject is varied, and located in many different places on the web. This book will put everything under one flat and firm roof, compartmentalizing the information into different rooms, in one enlightening house.

It will detail the legislative requirements that exist around shipping container homes and inform you where these ready-made floors and walls can be sourced. It will consider the myriad of benefits living in a shipping container home offers, but will also present some of the associated difficulties and challenges.

This book will take you through the steps of creating your own home by adapting these readily available resources, and it will give guidance on designing your own internal living spaces in these flexible shells. It will look at matters such as heating, plumbing, air conditioning, insulation, and decoration.

By following the guidance in this book, those looking to enter the market for their own shipping container home will have an advantage over others who are scrolling through the internet trying to find relevant information. It will provide a sure and certain account of the processes to follow, which are reliable and simple to use.

When you reach the end of this book, you will have a detailed and informed understanding of the subject, whether a shipping container home is something you wish to build for yourself, you wish to move into one ready for occupation, or you simply want to develop your knowledge of this growing trend.

Chapter 1: What Is A Shipping Container Home?

Bricks, wood, breeze blocks, canvas, wattle and daub…modern house building can be traced back to the Romans, who developed a way of cementing blocks together which strengthened their structures. Iron age homes in Europe were created by sinking giant posts into the ground, filling the gaps with wattle – a combination of reeds and twines knotted together, and daubed on clay. That process still exists today and was popular in the seventeen and early eighteen hundreds.

In Europe, stone was – and is – a well-loved building tool, but prefabricated houses with lightweight metal frames are also growing in popularity…in fact, the range of options for building a house is extensive. Most recently onto the scene has come one of the most obvious and smartest house-building materials yet.

What could this material be? It's actually quite an obvious solution. The thing is, the simplest of ideas are often overlooked by us; we tend to overcomplicate things. So, let's try to think simply.

We typically like our houses to be rectangular and solid to best utilize the lots in which they are built. We want a strong, stable object, ideally rectangular. It's probably also best for our material to be easily movable and relatively cheap. But where to find such an object? The answer is so blindingly simple: a shipping container.

In this chapter, we will look at how shipping containers became a fashionable way of creating a home, but firstly, let us make clear exactly what we mean when we talk about a shipping container home.

What Is A Shipping Container Home?

This question does not need a particularly long answer. A shipping container home is a home made from shipping containers. They can be combined to make two or three-story homes, or linked to make Lego-like bungalows. Later, we will see an example of a home constructed of nine boxes laid three on three on three. Indeed, the flexibility these containers offer is limited only by the regulations that surround them (more on that later) and the space their owners can utilize.

As a side note, shipping containers have their own unit of measurement, which is called a TEU (it stands for "twenty-foot equivalent unit"). One TEU is equal to one standard twenty-foot shipping container.

Early Examples

You might assume that this kind of home is extremely recent, a product of the last couple of years. Well, yes and no. One of the first of this new type of dwelling appeared in Brisbane, Australia in 2011.

Todd and Di Miller bought some land with the initial plan of renovating a run-down traditional house that was already built. They made a start, but then disaster struck. Severe floods damaged the property and their insurance did not cover all the repairs. The Millers did their best during the following year, but their dream home was rapidly turning into a nightmare. Then, Todd had a moment of inspiration. They considered the ways of going about creating their perfect house and realized that they simply did not have the money…for a traditional structure, that is. However, they could afford a few shipping containers. These would be cheap, quick to put together, and the recycling element made them a choice that was environmentally friendly as well.

Given the recent floods, the Queensland authorities insisted that the property be flood-proof, a characteristic (unsurprisingly) possessed by the containers. The local authorities approved the design, and the pair decided to buy new, ready-made containers. They paid $90,000 for the pre-painted containers complete with pine floors and other necessary materials – only $90,000 for a luxury four-bedroom home.

Here's the thing: In no way does their home look like it is constructed from shipping containers (thirty-one of them, to be exact). The ground floor features a double garage, an office, a pool room, a home gym, and an art studio. The second floor is made up of eleven containers put together to create an open plan living room and kitchen, three bedrooms, a bathroom, and a study. Then, on the top floor is the master bedroom, complete with a walk-in wardrobe, en suite bathroom, and terrace.

Although the Millers' home is considered one of the first shipping container homes, their story is not the beginning of the shipping container's journey from junk to building material.

In 1987, Phillip Clark filed a patent for converting a shipping container into a home – or "habitable building" as he referred to it. The patent office must have been a little shocked, because it took two years for the registered plans to be accepted. For those whose interest has been spiked, and who fancy a bit of historical investigation, the patent is US4854094A!

Even he was not the first, though, because in the 1970s, a UK architect wrote his university thesis on re-using shipping containers and turning them into homes. So, was that the beginning of the shipping container home?

Nope! We need to go back further still, to 1962, when the Insbrandtsen Company filed a patent for the first shipping container home of all, listing Christopher Betjemann as the inventor.

However, the fact that it was only recently that we might spy a collection of containers with a front door and attractive shrubbery (as opposed to the weeds which grow around most containers left behind wire fences close to the dockyards) gives us a clue that, as an idea, this was one slow to take root. Only in the last couple of years might we have been invited to have a cup of tea in a room that once carried cargo across the ocean.

But Why?

At this point, you might be wondering why even bother making homes out of shipping containers. It's not like there are that many sitting around, right? Aren't they being used for shipping things?

Actually, one of the reasons for the sudden push to create shipping container homes is the availability of shipping containers. The slightly concerning (actually, the potentially climate-changing) fact is that in the US alone, there is a surplus of over five million shipping containers. Some of them are re-used or shipped back to where they originated, but many just sit rusting away.

Unfortunately, there are not that many things to be done with a second-hand shipping container. Option one is to sail them into a convenient Pacific storm and let them drop off the container ship and sink down to pollute the oceans. This happens more often than we might wish to believe. A better option is to re-use them, but at this point, there are far more shipping containers sitting around than the shipping industry can possibly use. Therefore, if they are to be re-used, it has to be as something else. A great option, then, is to use them to build homes. They can provide shelter and comfort for people rather than going to waste and junking up our planet.

Undoubtedly, some people will suggest simply melting the shipping containers down, but to do so requires twenty times as much energy as simply converting them to homes.

So really, converting shipping containers to homes is the best option for people and for the planet. We will look into this, and some other benefits of shipping container homes in a later chapter. For now, let's just say that we hope these homes are here to stay.

Chapter Summary

In this chapter:

- We have identified what a shipping container home is.

- We have delved a little into the history of shipping container homes.

- We have seen the environmental benefit of using shipping containers for housing.

In the next chapter, we will look at some of the legal issues you will need to be aware of before creating your own home using containers.

Chapter 2: Licenses & Laws

If you want to build a shipping container home, you can't simply drive down to the local dockyard with a couple of friends and a trailer and pick up a few containers, stop at the nearest home store for some new curtains and a couple potted plants, and be on your way.

In this chapter, we'll take a look at some of the legislation around the world concerning the use of these handy building blocks.

Legislation In The USA

There is not a quick to-do list that you can check items off of to get a shipping container home up and running in the US. It is very much down to how each state – and even city – considers things. However, we can offer some basic guidance in taking the first steps.

Building Codes

These are the minimum standards every home must meet in the US and are in place for the protection of the inhabitants of the home. It is important to study them as they apply for the state in which you plan to build your shipping container home.

Therefore, any residential (or, for that matter, commercial) unit needs to have its building plans approved by the appropriate state authority. The first step is to apply to have the plans examined. Once the plans are approved and you have built your home, the building will need to pass safety checks.

The clear message is to consult a local architect, or at least one who knows the area in which you are aiming to build. It is also best to use an architect who is familiar with this type of structure, which shouldn't prove too difficult to find: as the trend grows, more and more companies have agents with specialist knowledge in the field. This expertise can be really important when it comes to getting the plans approved.

There are a few problems even well-prepared home builders can face at the Building Code stage:

• Shipping containers are designed to spread their weight load to the strong rails and posts upon which the structure is created. This is not always true of a house.

• Shipping containers are not insulated, unless specially treated. Insulation is an important factor in building design, because to get approval, not only is the safety of the inhabitants a consideration, but the wastage that may result from heating an ineffectively insulated structure has to be considered as well.

• Neighbors may object. Although they are growing in popularity, most people still have little knowledge of what a shipping container home really looks like, and how attractive in can be. Many will picture rusting wrecks covered in graffiti and chipped paintwork. Their objection may kill your plans unless they are properly presented.

• Finally, and this is something especially hard to deal with, many inspectors know little to nothing about shipping container homes. This can make getting building code approval a real lottery. The chances of drawing a winning ticket are so much better if you have inside information, which is what your local architect can provide.

Getting A Building Permit

Again, there is no magic recipe for success in earning a building permit, but those who do their homework increase their chances.

• Communication: Start a dialogue with the local authority representative as soon as you can. Be open and up front, explain your intentions and why you are following this route.

- Information: Build up a dossier of the benefits of building a shipping container home, but do not be afraid to show that you are aware of any pitfalls and have a solution ready should they occur. Do some solid investigation locally for any other container homes that have been built, and also find out about the range of home building materials in operation in the region. If there are none, then warning bells should sound; somebody will eventually be the person who breaks the local mold, but achieving that is much harder than following in another's footsteps. In looking for a range of building materials, look for eco homes, homes constructed of tires, dome housing, cave housing, underground housing, and so forth. These are rare to find, but evidence of them in the area might mean that the local authority is open minded.

- Be flexible about your destination. Before you buy your plot of land, make sure that you are not wasting your money and have some reserves in mind. Generally, this kind of housing will stand a greater chance of approval if it is away from a well-established area or is in an area where there are other kinds of experimental housing.

Legislation In The UK

Planning permission is a must in the UK. As with the US, a good local architect will be worth their weight in gold with an application for something as unusual as a shipping container home. They will have an idea of how the local council (who make the decisions on these matters) will regard the concept, and to whom you should speak.

If there are neighbors nearby, it is a good idea to meet with them and show them clear pictures of what the final building will look like. Also, be prepared to talk about any possible disruption, stressing the speed at which a container home can go up.

Getting planning permission in the UK is easier than it used to be, because there is a drive to create new housing. On the other hand, the real power under the current government (and the last few, in fact) lies with the big building companies.

If planning permission is granted, there will be regular building work inspections while the home is being built.

General Legislation

The process for getting permission to build your new home varies from country to country, with variations within those countries themselves. However, we can summarize the information into a couple of general points.

• Contact your local planning office before incurring any financial outlay. This can be done directly or through a professional intermediary such as an architect or lawyer.

• Safety is the primary concern in most cases, so expect to have your building closely monitored.

• Work with neighbors, keeping them in the loop as to the progress of the build, to ensure a smooth passage.

Chapter Summary

In this chapter, we have considered the legal considerations for building a shipping container home. Our conclusion is that there is no set legislation, but that it depends on the local area. A summary of our best advice is:

• Communicate with everyone involved or affected by your new home.

• Get professional advice along the way. This will make the process smoother and more likely to succeed, even though it is an additional cost.

• Remember insulation! You are unlikely to succeed with your application without evidence of how this will be provided.

• Safety is key. Keeping this at the forefront of your thinking will help to improve your chances of success.

- The more isolated an area, the more likely you are to be successful with your application; evidence of other creative designs using non-standard building materials indicates that the local authority is open-minded about home design.

In the next chapter, we will consider ways to source the shipping containers for your planned new home.

Chapter 3: Sourcing Containers

In this chapter, we will cover the facts and figures concerning getting ahold of the containers that could become your future home.

Types Of Containers

There are two main types of standard containers, although personalized sizes are made by some companies. The standard sizes are both eight feet wide. One length is 20 feet, giving an overall square footage of 160 square feet (the TEU mentioned previously). The other is double the length at 40 feet, giving an overall square footage of 320 square feet. This is called two TEU.

To give you an idea of size: There have recently been some interesting reports about a 100 square foot apartment in New York. This is a studio, with no separate bathroom (just a curtain to separate it from the living space) and little storage space. This would be about the same as trying to live inside one shipping container. Realistically, it is too small to live in comfortably. The smallest square footage that is realistic is 240; just enough for a bedroom and attached bathroom, a living area, and a kitchen, utility, and storage area.

Of course, most people are going to want a little more space than the bare minimum. Even a small house will require three to six TEUs for a square footage somewhere between 480 and 960. For a medium or large home, you will need even more.

As of 2018, you can expect to pay, for a basic second-hand container in decent condition, between $1,500 and $3,000 for one TEU, and between $3,600 and $5,000 for the larger option (which can be called two TEU, although this makes it a bit confusing when discussing how many containers you want). If you want containers that are already insulated or have been otherwise modified for home use, expect to pay more. You can avoid higher prices by choosing to modify the containers yourself, as some container sellers will provide conversion kits.

Acquiring Shipping Containers

This is both as easy as pie and as tricky as cooking a three-course cordon bleu meal. The easy side is that a quick search online will yield pages upon pages of container sellers. Of course, some of these sellers are not as reputable as others and most of the inventory is going to be chipped and rusted. The good news is that there are still plenty of great options.

Pre-Constructed Container Homes

Fortunately, for those who would like to have this option, it is straight forward enough to find a company that will send you your home ready-made. Logical Homes, with bases in Los Angeles, California; Houston, Texas; New York; and New Jersey, is one such organization. It opens its website page with a quote from Albert Einstein, which rather cleverly sums up the concept of container homes:

"…Any intelligent fool can make things bigger, more complex, and more violent. It takes a touch of genius – and a lot of courage – to move in the opposite direction."

Logical Homes takes an ethical approach to home building, considering homelessness and the environment in its developments. It provides 16 standard home designs to provide cleverly designed, space-saving homes, minimizing the size of the plot it is necessary to buy. Each of these designs has a set floor plan but offers some customization when it comes to color schemes and materials used. Only 15 of the designs are meant to be complete living spaces (the other is only 160 square feet and offers no bedroom), ranging in size from 320 to 3,580 square feet and ranging in price from $60,000 to $430,000.

For an example of the possibilities, Logical Homes offers a single story three-bedroom house with twin garages on either side of the front porch. The front entrance opens on a den, which leads on to a large open-plan kitchen, living room, and dining room, which runs the length of the house. Off to either side are the bedrooms. On one side, two bedrooms share a "Jack and Jill" bathroom, while the master bedroom on the other side has its own en suite. There is even space for an office.

And that's just one example from the range of prefabricated shipping container homes available from Logical Homes. And of course, Logical Homes is just one of the numerous companies that can supply one of these ready-built homes.

These companies will usually do everything that is needed. They will transport the home, put it together, and make it ready for use. The thing to note is that the convenience offered by this option will come at a cost.

Pre-Fabricated Do-It-Yourself Containers

A second option is to mix do-it-yourself with containers that are pretty much ready to be slotted together. Again, there are many companies out there that can supply everything needed, including a company called LOT-EK, which specializes in Container Home Kits. These kits include plans for a shipping container home that can range in size from 1,000 to 3,000 square feet. You can choose between one, two, three, and four bedrooms, and can even choose to add on a pool and pool house, tool shed, or carport. You just pay for the designs that fit the plans you have for your new home, and LOT-ET supplies them.

It then becomes a matter of putting them together. This is a job that requires specialist support and equipment, but the final construction is not overly complicated and so it is possible to shop around and find builders who can do the job cheaply. A total cost for their skills is likely to fall somewhere between $10,000 and $15,000.

A Complete Self-Build Approach

For those with the skills, time, and inclination, you can build a home completely from scratch. The next chapter will look in some detail at the way to do this.

It is often cheaper for a cargo company to buy a new container, than to ship their second-hand ones back to where they are needed. This means that there exists a great deal of containers in a full range of conditions waiting to be snapped up.

Containers contain codes, usually painted on their sides, which allow the would-be builder to trace the age and usage of a particular container. Therefore, you can ensure that it has not been used to transport hazardous goods. You can select containers that are in good condition, and negotiate prices with the seller.

By their nature, containers are designed to be easily shipped. Once you've purchased your containers, you can set up a plan for this to be done, find contractors who can remove panels and insert windows and the like, do the cleaning and painting yourself, and (depending on your skills or those of your family and friends) get them floored and insulated.

This is a lot of work (although much less than building a traditional brick home from scratch) and much of that work is difficult. However, the result is a home built exactly to your specifications, and one which you have the satisfaction of knowing you built yourself.

Chapter Summary

In this chapter, we have seen that there are many ways to source containers for our homes. You can:

• Choose to purchase a pre-fabricated shipping home and have the materials transported and put together by a specialist company.

• Purchase plans from a specialist company and have them oversee the building of your home. You will still be responsible for labor and material costs.

• Adopt a completely do-it-yourself approach. Make the plans, buy the containers, hire the labor, etc.

Chapter 4: How To Build A Home

This chapter will look at the home building process for a shipping container home. Doing this is exciting, easier than might be feared, but is still a challenge. We cannot emphasize enough the value of seeking advice from professional experts, like architects to assist with design and planning, lawyers to ensure that all legal requirements are met, logistics companies to assist with the planning of the delivery of containers on site, builders to help with the heavy-duty elements of construction, and specialist tradesmen, such as plumbers and electricians, to assist with key tasks that you may not possess the skills to complete alone.

Doing Your Groundwork

These are tips and suggestions that you should follow before you begin. Making sure that you carried out your personal "due diligence" will make things easier in the long run, so don't skip it, even though you may be eager to get started.

Choosing Your Container

Yes, you can buy new, but you can save a substantial amount by buying a container that has only completed one trip. Such a container is likely to be in good condition, and depending on what it stored, clean inside. However, if you choose to buy a container that is not new, make sure you see it in person. You'll be spending $20,000 to $30,000 on containers alone, and so the money for a trip to see the containers is money well spent. After all, you would never spend $30,000 on a nearly new car without seeing it first.

Spending a little time researching the marketplace is also worthwhile. There are, for example, some containers, often referred to as "cubes" that are much taller than a standard design. Some are longer than others. Generally, a large container is going to cost more than a smaller one, but not twice the price for twice the size. Knowing the range of containers on the market could save you time and money later, reducing alteration costs and providing a better fit for what you require.

Doing The Legal Eagle Bit

As we pointed out earlier, different countries, different states or regions, even different towns in the same county could have different rules and regulations on, for example, fire retardants or waste disposal. A little time spent reading up or speaking with an expert – that could just be somebody from the local authority where you hope to build – can save a lot of later heartache.

Think as well about the climate in which you are hoping to build. Is there an extreme range of temperatures? Are snow and ice likely? Will it get tremendously hot in the summer months? Is it close to the coast where salty air might lead to greater chances of rust?

Containers are versatile and built to withstand all that the oceans can throw at them, so they do make excellent materials for building a house…but an idyllic home in the English countryside is going to be experiencing a far different climate than one in the Mojave Desert or the northern reaches of Newfoundland. For example, when it comes to insulation, you need to consider factors such as condensation, which will be worse in colder conditions.

Hiring The Most Suitable Contractor

Again, there are many, many builders and developers who will gladly assist with the construction of a shipping container home. Mostly, they will a good job. But it is definitely the case that any construction job becomes more complicated the more contractors are at work.

This can involve, for example, the insulators not being able to start work because the team who will cut the containers for windows and doors is behind. It will be you that pays the cost here.

If possible, it is worth trying to find a contractor who will take charge of all the work. It then becomes their responsibility to ensure that their teams are best employed. They will have the motivation to make it work, because the quicker they can finish the job, the sooner they can make a start on their next client's requirements.

Understanding Container Dynamics

Knowledge of how a container works will help you with the design process and save you potential time, money, and disappointment further down the line. Employing an architect with expert knowledge is really worthwhile. For example, the side walls are the load bearing sections of most containers. Therefore, deciding to cut a large window out of one of those sides means that the strength of the container is compromised, and this will need to be compensated for in the design.

A further consideration is the welding involved in making the containers stable and strong. This is expensive and a specialized skill, so the less you need to have done in your new home, the better value for money it will represent.

Keeping Expectations Realistic

You are going to save quite a bit of money by building your home from containers, but it is not a completely cost-free exercise. You need to be realistic about the budget you allocate for the task. Anybody you talk to who has built their own home will tell you that hidden and unexpected costs often show up. Even if you are following a very cost-effective approach to building your home, you still need a contingency fund in place and you still need to expect to pay a little more than your original estimates.

Plumbing Factors...And Others

It is best to have your plumbing inserts ready-made before constructing the property, and certainly before any internal work. The same applies for wiring. Designing a house can be huge fun, and it makes sense for you to input your own desires and requirements, but as we keep emphasizing, you need the opinion of a proper architect with knowledge of building a shipping container home. Not only will this person consider all of the things you might forget, or not even know about, but if there is a problem, it will be their job to sort it out rather than you having to muddle your way through fixing the issue.

Don't Forget The Wind

There are a number of really strong advantages to having a metal home; waterproofing and strength are just two that come quickly to mind. However, your home will basically be a series of metal boxes. And when the wind hits a metal box, the external noise is magnified inside.

This should not be a problem if you think big about insulation, sound-proofing, and how the angle of the building can cope with the prevailing wind, especially where your location is exposed to the elements. You can also consider your plot as a whole, thinking about ways in which you can utilize vegetation to act as a wind barrier and so cut out noise.

Once you've completed your groundwork, checked out the design, sourced your containers, and contracted your experts, you can move onto the next stage in the construction of your shipping container home.

Buying Your Plot

You've done your research, presented your plan, and had it approved. Now, it's time to start the real work. The next step is buying a plot. It could be a plot with an existing home on it that will be knocked down before starting, or it could be a completely new plot for which planning permission exists for a residential dwelling.

Again, conditions depend on both national and regional legislation. However, as a broad principle, the first step once you have found the land you would like is to check the zoning ordinances for the area. Check to see if there are any restrictions and consider the future, as well. If a six-lane freeway is going to be built nearby over the next ten years, starting the month after you start building your own home, that plot of land is probably not the best.

Check out the surroundings. Is there a pig farm nearby? Does that factory over the hill belch out noxious fumes, and if so, in what direction does the prevailing wind blow?

You also need to be aware of natural hazards. If the area is prone to flooding, getting planning permission will be difficult, and the cost of building defenses could be both prohibitive and futile. Insurance costs will be high. Test the soil and see if there is landfill nearby which might have polluted the land. If your plot is on a hill, check for land movement, which could cause the foundations of your home to crack and collapse.

Ensure that there will be no major problems connecting to utilities, or if that will prove difficult, consider the costs of alternatives.

Finally, check out access. Sometimes new parcels of land have to be accessed by crossing other people's property. If this is the case, an easement is needed, and it needs to be official and recorded. Find out whether neighbors will have access across your land or whether it is a part of a natural footpath or bridleway. Also check whether roads accessing your land are officially maintained, or if it is down to landowners to keep them drivable.

A Firm Foundation

The next stage on the journey is to decide on the foundations. You can't simply plop your containers down on your land. Foundations can be made of many materials, but most builders will recommend concrete because it is cheap, and the containers can simply be welded to it.

A consideration is whether to create a basement, which is a great facility to own, but not cheap. A better alternative for those on a budget might be to create a crawl space which can be used for storage.

Getting Out The Credit Card

Getting a loan to build your home will, like so much else in this process, depend on where you live. However, because the building will not be a traditional structure, getting a mortgage might prove more difficult than you expect. It is important to have funding in place, be it cash or a loan.

So, you have located and bought your containers, considering the factors listed in previous chapters. Any modifications are best made before the containers are transported to your building plot. Cutting heavy metal takes a fair amount of time with a hacksaw and you would go through too many blades to make it economical! Heavy duty cutting equipment will be needed, and there are limitations, because of safety, as to where such cutting can take place. Most systems will employ a plasma cutter, which both cuts and melts the metal. However, this requires an air compressor and is not a do-it-yourself job. Proper training and qualifications are needed to handle such equipment.

Any modifications that are made to a container will compromise its strength. Therefore, reference needs to be made to a structural engineer to ensure that any changes are safe and practical. Once again, a specialist architect is likely to be your best option in the long run. This passes responsibility and duty of care to a qualified professional; however keen and talented an amateur you might be, mistakes are easily made, and the consequences could be that your new home has to be ripped down before you even move in. Even worse, it could collapse.

Smaller modifications, such as window frames and door frames are also better done offsite, where there is more space to carry out works, and the process will cause no disturbance to the neighborhood.

Once the modifications have been made to your containers, it is time to organize transportation to your site.

Time To Play Legos

Once they have arrived, putting together the different units should be a relatively quick job. With all modifications made, they should slot together easily enough and be quickly secured to your foundations.

You connect them just as they would be attached to a ship. This means locking the corners together. Since they will not be disembarked any time soon – we hope – additional strength is ensured by welding them securely together. Each container is capable of supporting up to 57,000 pounds – plenty more than that of an average household, so there should be no problem at all with stability and security. However, you must remember that strength will have been weakened by any modifications you have made.

It Needs A Roof

Although shipping containers are not open to the elements, their integrity can be lost when they are attached together. The biggest problem is likely to be a build up of water on the top, which could lead to fairly rapid damage to the structure. It is best, and not overly expensive, to add a roof. This not only allows for safe water flow, but could, for example, allow you to add on solar panels to power the home. In many countries, grants are available for this kind of work, and sometimes excess energy can be sold back to the national grid. There are also, depending on global location, many companies who fit a solar roof for next to nothing in return for taking the long-term income from selling excess energy back to the network.

Doors And Windows

Right now, you have a bunch of containers with holes in them slotted together and attached to your foundation. Your doors and windows come next. These should simply slot into the spaces made for them. Then, frames are added to ensure security, safety, and proper sealing.

Insulation

This is a must. The containers will get very cold in winter and exceptionally hot in the summer. There are various choices from which to choose when it comes to insulation. These include foam layers inside and out, or a mixture of the old and the new by attaching a natural insulator such as thatch. Perhaps the best and easiest option is to use some ceramic-based insulating paint. This is the stuff used by NASA in its space program, so it ought to cope with anything from a Russian winter to a Saudi Arabian summer without breaking a sweat.

Indeed, an advantage of this type of insulation is that it protects against moisture inside and out. Mold, mildew, and rust will be prevented from forming and the application is simple, sticking well to the metal walls of your container home.

The Nitty-Gritty

Plumbing, electrics, water, and gas go in next. The locations for these will have been decided at the planning stage, and cuts for pipes and wires will already be in place. It is important to remember that for these services, a qualified expert needs to be employed. Fitting wiring is not a do-it-yourself job. Similarly, if gas is to be fitted, the risks of not using a qualified engineer are not even worth a second of consideration – just employ an expert.

Since one of the reasons for choosing a shipping container home is the environmental benefits of such a house, the solar panels and opportunities for natural light, insulation, and so forth are likely to be high in the thinking of owners. An expert can be helpful in these areas, as well.

Flooring

The next stage is to get down your flooring. Many containers come with plywood flooring, but this is best ripped out unless you are sure of its history. Containers are often sprayed with insecticides, which can settle into the wood and can be harmful to your health.

In addition, flooring is one of the most important parts of a home, and can help with heating, cooling, and insulation. Spending a little time and perhaps a small part of your budget getting the ideal flooring is a cost-effective expense.

Decoration

All that is left is to decorate your new home and fill it with lovely furniture. You can build your pool, prepare the BBQ area in the garden, get fencing done, or whatever you need to add the final touches to your home.

Chapter Summary

In this chapter, we have considered the steps to building our own shipping container home.

- Plenty of preparation and groundwork is important.

- Modifications need to be made before the containers can be transported.

- Make use of professional expertise for key tasks.

Next, we will consider in detail the benefits – and any down sides – of building your own shipping container home.

Chapter 5: Pros & Cons

Now it is time to make a detailed assessment of the advantages and disadvantages of building – and living in – a shipping container home.

Advantages Of Shipping Container Homes

The following list identifies some of the main benefits of owning a home of this kind. They are not presented in any particular order, because your home –and what you want in it – will be individual to you. What is appealing to one person may be well down the shopping list of somebody different.

Stylish And Chic

Some people rather negatively regard something new and trendy as a fad, and not something to last. We only have to look at the range of styles of homes to see that trends might change, but the creations they produce hang around.

In current thinking, there is little more fashionable than a shipping container home. Practical, affordable, and environmentally friendly (we will look at these benefits in more detail shortly), the homes are everything the modern buyer is seeking. In addition, because a container is a blank canvas, the outside can be shaped to reflect pretty much any style that appeals to you.

Affordability

Container homes might have been around for 50 years, but it is only in the last four or five that they have started to become bigger business. This means that there is still uncertainty around the savings a container home provides when compared with more traditional structures. Certainly, using prefabricated containers, or pre-built houses is easier, but more expensive. Comparing new build with new build, there are substantial savings to be had, and a large do-it-yourself project could be up to a third – perhaps even more – cheaper.

Easy To Build

We covered in the previous chapter that building a container home does require some work. But this is nothing compared to building a brick or stone construction. Putting the home together is also incredibly quick. Nobody enjoys a building site in their neighborhood, and the speed with which a container home can be completed is likely to cause far less stress and unhappiness among our new neighbors than spending a year building a traditional home.

In fact, from start to finish – given a good run with the legal side of things – the process can be as short as just a couple of months.

Flexibility

Because, in many ways, your new home will be modular in design, the sky is the limit when it comes to design factors. If you want two or three stories, no problem. If you want open-space living, it can be incorporated. Fancy a courtyard pool, surrounded on all sides by your home? Go ahead!

And there are so many businesses who will sell containers, that finding materials is no problem at all.

Environmentally Friendly

As we have stated before, there are huge environmental benefits to building a home from shipping containers. Their metal, as long as it is properly insulated, makes them good for holding in both heat and cool air when needed. They are easily adapted to accept alternative energy – because many are built outside of main population centers, it is not just solar energy that can be building material leaves a much smaller carbon footprint than dragging them around the world to the right port ready to be filled with goods.

Creating Affordable And Accessible Housing

By building your own shipping container home, you are contributing to the growth of the industry. As industries grow, their goods become cheaper as better ways of production and the savings of competition come into play.

Finding affordable housing is difficult in many parts of the world. There are issues in countries hit by natural disasters, where temporary, quick-build homes are needed after floods and earthquakes. In the west, the increase in property prices rules out many people from owning their own homes. In the UK, for example, the average age at which a person owns their first property has increased three years over the past 20 years. This may seem like a small increase, but it is significant. It means that it's taking longer for people to accumulate the funds necessary for home ownership, as well as highlights the lack of affordable housing available.

In fact, there are many people who will never get the chance to own their own properties. Innovative ideas such as container homes could provide a solution, and as prices fall from their already low point, so the option becomes available to more and more people.

Disadvantages Of Shipping Container Homes

Limits Of The Container

Not too many people want their homes to have curves, but if that appeals to you, then a container home will be difficult to use. The boxy shapes mean that a boxy final construction is likely. Certainly, the containers can be arranged to avoid long straight walls, but domes and turrets are not on the agenda.

Another factor to consider is that a big truck is needed to deliver a container, and at least 100 feet of maneuvering space is required to get the truck in and out and safely unload the container from it. It might be difficult to have the containers delivered to a suburban neighborhood. Then again, as we have explained, shipping container homes work best on the edge of a town or city, or in the countryside, so this issue should not pose too much of a problem for most.

Cost And Resale

This is a tricky one. Certainly, a newly built shipping container home as compared to a newly built traditional home means that there will be savings. However, most people do not buy newly built homes. They buy existing houses that have already been lived in. There are very few container home versions of these second-hand properties, and plenty of traditional homes for sale.

Excluding the obvious advantages of moving into a home you have built and designed yourself, and to your own specifications, the saving presented by a newly built shipping container home as compared to an existing, previously lived in house, is much less impressive. However, into this complicated formula needs to be added the changes – decorative and perhaps structural – you will have to pay for in a house that does not completely fit your needs or desires.

Another factor to consider is resale. The market is still too small and too new to know how resale prices will hold up for container homes. Although the traditional housing market can be volatile, there has been a generally strongly upward trend across the globe (with the odd dip). Only time will tell whether those who have taken the step into the alternative will see the same benefits in term of property value increases.

Chapter Summary

In this chapter, we have considered the benefits of living in a shipping container home, and also looked at some of the down sides.

• Shipping container homes are stylish, affordable, easy to build, and environmentally friendly. You also have many design options.

• There are limits to the way you can design your home. For example, you will not be able to create a turret unless you choose to add other materials to your design.

• Shipping container homes might not be less expensive than traditional homes on the market. It is also unknown how easily they can be sold should you decide to move.

In the next chapter, we will assuage any fears you have about design options, consider some of the remarkable ways people have created their fashionable new homes, and offer a bit of advice about design before you move forward.

Chapter 6: The Many Choices

We have looked at the processes you must go through to build your home. You know shipping container homes are affordable, good for the environment, and easy to build. The only issue we haven't completely cleared up is the issue of design. Shipping containers are boxes. And they're made of corrugated metal. Are you going to be looking at a metal wall? Is there anything your home can be other than a big box? Fear not! Now it's time to consider some of the clever, ingenious, and frankly astonishing ways innovative owners have turned simple shipping containers into stunning homes.

A Few Tips

While it might seem impossible to envision a beautiful home made out of old metal boxes, the reality isn't that difficult to achieve when you bear a few things in mind:

You are not bound to using recycled shipping containers as your only building material. Mix the containers with brick or wood accents. Add containers to an existing structure. Get creative!

You are limited by your imagination. If you go into the process with the mindset that you can only have a boring, rectangular house, that's what you'll end up with. If you plan to design your own home, feel free to create the crazy shapes you want. Let your architect know what you have in mind. If it's possible, they can make it happen.

When all else fails: You can embrace the industrial vibe of the shipping container. Use it to inspire design elements that make the space cool, funky, and cohesive.

Mixing It Up

Something that people get into their heads when they hear about shipping container homes is that they'll be living in a big metal box if they choose such an option. However, it's very unlikely to find a shipping container home that does not incorporate some other building materials. Okay, well that's one worry eased, but what about the effect of these other materials on the home's affordability? Or its environmentally-friendliness?

No need to worry! These other materials can be salvaged and recycled, keeping your shipping container home both inexpensive and good for the environment.

For example, in 2017 in St. Charles, Missouri, Zach and Brie Smithey created the first shipping container home in the area. But their house doesn't look like a big metal box plopped down in a residential neighborhood. In fact, from the front, their house mostly looks to be made of brick!

The frame of their home is created by eight shipping containers, with four forming the bottom floor and four forming the top. In the end, the house cost them $135,000 to build for a whopping 3,100 square feet. How did they accomplish this? By keeping an eye out for materials they could salvage or recycle.

The front of their home is clad in brick left over from a friend's home remodel, and sports upside-down antique arched windows salvaged from an old church. Inside, baseboards and crown moldings made from the randomly cut boards of old pallets, frames created by rope pulled from the muddy banks of the Mississippi River, birdbaths refashioned as sinks, and dozens of other recycled materials (including combine chains and a conch shell!) live in harmony.

The Smitheys left some parts of the shipping container frame exposed, mixing the corrugated metal with other elements to create a whimsical and awe-inspiring home. So don't worry. Not only is mixing it up allowed, it's encouraged!

Unusual Designs

Although the Smithey house in St. Charles is innovative in its use of salvaged and recycled materials, it is quite conventional (for a shipping container home) in another way: it is pretty much a large cube. There's nothing inherently wrong with this; in fact, the design suits the home's neighborhood well. But what if you want something a little more exciting, perhaps even something a little crazy?

Well, you can have that, too! All you have to do is take a look at the work of designer James Whitaker to know that shipping containers don't have to be square. In 2010 in Germany's Black Forest, Whitaker designed Hechingen Studio, an office building for a German advertising agency. Its design has been compared to a starburst and a sea anemone, and is quite striking.

Whitaker has now designed a similar building – this time a home – to be built just outside California's Joshua Tree National Park. The design features containers bursting out from a center point, facing all directions, even skyward. Solar panels will provide electricity for the 2,100 square-foot, three-bedroom residence.

Although construction has just begun and the home is not expected to be completed until late 2018 at least, Whitaker's digital renderings of the finished product serve to awe and inspire. The moral of this story? Shipping container homes don't have to be square. They don't have to be boring. They can be as crazy and as innovative as your mind allows.

Industrial Chic

Up to this point, we've presented you with ways to keep your shipping container home from looking like…well, a shipping container home. Now, let's consider for a moment that a shipping container home looking like what it is might not be such a bad thing!

There is an argument to be made for embracing the corrugated metal of the shipping container from a design standpoint. It's not for everyone, but industrial interior design has grown in popularity over the years. Often, industrial style includes cultivating a kind of raw, unfinished look by displaying the parts of building that tend to be hidden. It often includes a lot of wood and metal, as well as exposed pipes and ductwork. What better design for a shipping container home?

For example, there is a green (both figuratively and literally) shipping container home in Flagstaff, Arizona. It was designed by Ecosa Institute and completed in 2011. This home makes no secret of the fact that it is made from shipping containers. Rather, it embraces the fact. The metal of the containers has been left exposed, although painted a mint green. The floors are cement with a walnut finish and the interior incorporates lots of metal and wood. Even the fencing is metal. And the design works. It has a cool, urban feel, but ample vegetation warms up the exterior and the interior manages to be cozy rather than clinical.

Take a look at some of the many shipping container homes that have embraced industrial style to celebrate the innovativeness of their building material. You might still be skeptical about showcasing the sea-tossed, weather-worn sides of your shipping containers, but you also might find that the industrial aesthetic is much more appealing than you imagined.

Another Few Tips

Hopefully, these examples have reassured you that you can make whatever you want of your shipping container home. The only thing left to do is start brainstorming about what you actually want! By this point, you've been introduced to so many concepts and available options, you might be unsure of where to start. To help you out, here are a few final tips for creating your shipping container home:

• Especially in smaller homes, incorporate lots of windows and natural light. This will open up the space and make it feel bigger than it is, even if you only use two or three containers.

• Alternatively, you can blur the lines between indoor and outdoor spaces. For example, you can create a courtyard surrounded by four shipping containers.

• Don't be afraid to let your shipping container show! Use plants to create an interesting juxtaposition between natural and industrial elements.

• If you plan to use other building materials in your home (which you probably do), try to salvage and recycle as much as possible. This will ensure that you don't blow your project budget AND that the environmentally-friendliness of your house doesn't go out the window.

• Most of all, CHOOSE WHAT IS BEST FOR YOU! This is your home, not anyone else's. Make the choices that best fit your needs. If you can't stand looking at metal walls, don't choose an industrial interior design.

Chapter Summary

In this chapter, we have illustrated some of the many ways in which clever thinking can turn box-shaped containers into innovative, interesting shapes to make homes that are practical but inventive, usable but eye catching.

• Homes can be created from just one simple container, or from many containers to create complex and aesthetically-pleasing shapes which enhance a neighborhood.

• Homes can be made of containers combined with more traditional materials for a touch of whimsy or left on their own to create an industrial look.

• Incorporate natural elements like light and vegetation into your home design, especially if you plan to adhere to a more industrial style. This will add contrast and interest to your home, as well as help it fulfill its potential.

• Salvage and recycle what building materials you can. This has two benefits: cost savings and environmental friendliness.

- No matter what advice we give about design, in the end, this is your home. Make it the home you want.

Conclusion

I hope that you have found this introduction to shipping container homes useful, and that if you were considering creating a home of your own using these versatile and easily obtained structures, your desire to do so is even stronger now.

Building a home such as this is environmentally sound, economically sensible, and aesthetically pleasing.

This book has covered some of the background of this kind of home, places from which it is possible to source shipping containers, and the sort of costs involved. It has explained the full range of this kind of home, from pre-fabricated, ready-made homes that simply slot into your plot to the do-it-yourself approach where everything is down to organization from the home owner.

The shipping container home trend is growing, and for those to whom this idea appeals, we strongly recommend getting in on the trend and creating a unique home that will be good for the planet, catch the eye of passers-by, and provide a practical, versatile, and original home.

Thank you again for purchasing this book and for letting us guide you through your exploration of the world of shipping container homes!

www.ingramcontent.com/pod-product-compliance
Lightning Source LLC
LaVergne TN
LVHW021141150125
801360LV00021B/352